BX

D1635974

Special thanks to our adviser:
Susan Kesselring, M.A., Literacy Educator
Rosemount–Apple Valley–Eagan (Minnesota) School District

It Never Rains in Antarctica

and Other Freaky Facts About Climate, Land, and Nature

by Barbara Seuling

illustrated by Ryan Haugen

PICTURE WINDOW BOOKS
Minneapolis, Minnesota

Editors: Christianne Jones and Emmeline Elliott
Designer: Abbey Fitzgerald
Page Production: Melissa Kes
Art Director: Nathan Gassman
The illustrations in this book were created digitally.

Picture Window Books
151 Good Counsel Drive
P.O. Box 669
Mankato, MN 56002-0669
877-845-8392
www.picturewindowbooks.com

Library of Congress Cataloging-in-Publication Data
Seuling, Barbara.
It never rains in Antarctica : and other freaky facts about climate,
land, and nature / by Barbara Seuling ; illustrated by Ryan Haugen.
p. cm.
Includes index.
ISBN 978-1-4048-4117-8 (library binding)
1. Earth sciences—Miscellanea—Juvenile literature. 2. Weather—
Miscellanea—Juvenile literature. 3. Curiosities and wonders—
Miscellanea—Juvenile literature. I. Haugen, Ryan, 1972- ill.
II. Title.
QE53.S485 2009
550—dc22   2008006334

Table of Contents

Dry and Hot, Dark and Cold:
Deserts and Caves

The sand on the beach of the Bay of Laig on the Isle of Eigg, Scotland, makes musical sounds when it is walked on. Nobody knows for sure what causes the sounds.

The Sahara is the largest desert in the world. It stretches across one-third of the African continent.

Only one-quarter of the Sahara Desert is covered by sand dunes. The rest is covered by mountains and plains.

Sand dunes in the Sahara can be up to 1,155 feet (352 m) high.

Many people lived in the Sahara Desert when it was a savanna thousands of years ago.

Early mapmakers wrote "Here Are Lions" to fill empty spaces on maps of the Sahara Desert.

The highest recorded temperature on Earth is 136.4 F (58.5 C), recorded in Al' Aziziyah (El Azizia), Libya.

There can be frost in the Sahara Desert. It is common in the mountains and the northern sand seas in winter.

The Sahara Desert has some areas that are below sea level.

In 1947, a storm in the Sahara Desert blew reddish dust everywhere. The dust was carried by the wind and deposited in the Swiss Alps, 1,000 miles (1,600 km) away. The dust turned the snow pink.

A windstorm in the 1930s blew 350 million tons (315 million metric tons) of dust from the western plains of the United States to the Atlantic Ocean.

People have lived in caves from the earliest times. Around 1200 B.C., Anasazi Indians built caves in cliffs in the southwestern United States. These caves were similar to apartments.

Caves have been used by many groups of people as natural refrigerators. A 4,000-year-old cave was discovered in Idaho that was used by Native Americans to store bison meat.

Long before air-conditioning was invented, the cool air from Howe Caverns in New York was forced above ground. The air cooled a hotel during the hot summer months.

The desert people of Tunisia built their houses underground. It was much cooler.

Some doctors once prescribed living in caves to people with tuberculosis, a disease of the lungs. The pure air and even temperatures were thought to be a healthful climate for them.

Paintings made during the Stone Age have been discovered in caves in Spain and France. The pictures record a way of life that existed long ago. They were perfectly preserved by the cave temperature and air.

Cave paintings found in the Sahara Desert in northern Africa show that elephants once roamed there.

In the Waitomo Cave in New Zealand, there are millions of tiny twinkling blue-green lights. The twinkling comes from the pulsing lights of thousands of glowworms.

One of the largest cave systems in the world, Carlsbad Caverns in New Mexico, was first explored by a cowboy. He thought he saw smoke coming out of the ground. The "smoke" turned out to be millions of bats coming out of the caves for their evening meal.

The Carlsbad Caverns' "Big Room" is 25 stories high. It is one-third of a mile (0.53 km) long and 250 feet (76 m) wide.

The Blue Grotto on the Isle of Capri in Italy is a sea cave. It was made by the steady pounding of seawater, wind, and rain. Sunlight, reflected through the water from an underwater cavity, fills the cave with blue light.

The world's largest sea cave is on the coast of Oregon. It has an opening 1,500 feet (457 m) long and 100 feet (31 m) high.

The porous rock of lava tube caves traps the cold. The temperature outside may be 100 F (38 C), but only 20 feet (6 m) below the ground the floors are frozen, and icicles hang from the ceiling.

Anthodites are rare formations of long thin needles of stone on cave ceilings. They grow about 1 inch (2.5 cm) in 7,000 years.

There are caves hollowed out of ice, rather than rock. These are formed as the ice melts. In Europe, there are underground ice caves, complete with frozen waterfalls and huge skating rinks.

Highs and Lows:
Mountains, Islands, and Water

At the North Pole, all directions are south.

There is no land at the North Pole. It is simply a mass of floating ice in the Arctic Ocean.

The continent of Antarctica is almost totally covered by ice that never melts. In some places the ice is 3 miles (4.8 km) thick.

If you count the submerged part, Mauna Loa is the tallest volcano in the world. The visible part is 13,680 feet (4,172 m) high. You can find Mauna Loa in Hawaii.

The highest mountain, counting from a land base, is Mount Everest in the Himalayas. It is 29,035 feet (8,856 m) high.

The deepest gorge in the world is the Great Gorge near Mount McKinley in Alaska. Including the depth of the glacier, the gorge is nearly 9,000 feet (2,745 m) deep.

In 1821, the first human recorded to set foot on the continent of Antarctica was John Davis. However, this fact wasn't discovered until 134 years later.

Greenland is the largest island in the world. Australia is bigger, but because of its huge size, it is considered a continent.

The International Date Line cuts around some of the islands in the South Pacific. You lose an entire day going from Samoa to Tonga, a journey of about 300 miles (480 km).

Mangrove trees are one of the few trees that can grow in salt water.

Some islands are built entirely of mangrove trees that have become entwined and entangled at their roots. These roots trap various small creatures and seeds and cause the land to slowly build up.

The lowest place in the world is the shore around the Dead Sea. It is about 1,300 feet (397 m) below sea level.

Half of the Netherlands lies below sea level. The Dutch have kept land dry by constructing dikes and then pumping out the seawater.

The greatest salt deposit on Earth is beneath the surface in Kansas. It is 400 feet (122 m) deep.

In Wieliczka, Poland, there is a city underground. It is carved out of salt. Seven levels are joined by a stairway carved from rock salt. The city has 186 miles (298 km) of passageways, including winding streets, churches, restaurants, a ballroom, a museum, and even horse-drawn railway cars.

Niagara Falls may disappear into Lake Erie one day. Every year the rushing waters wear away more of the cliff over which they flow. When all of the cliff rock is cut away, the falls will disappear.

The Tonle Sap River of Cambodia changes direction. It flows northward half of the year and southward the other half.

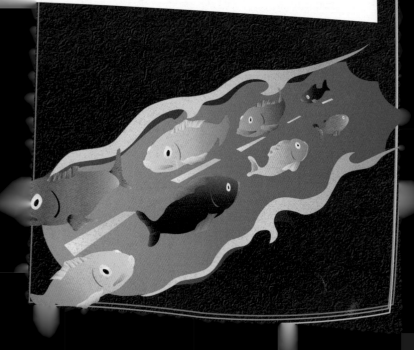

Koolau Falls on Oahu, Hawaii, looks like it is flowing upward. Powerful updrafts catch the water as it comes down over the cliffs and blow it back up.

The Amazon River of South America pushes so much fresh water into the Atlantic Ocean that the water remains fresh enough to drink 100 miles (160 km) from the mouth of the river.

The Yellow River in China has flooded so much farmland and killed so many people that it has been called China's Sorrow. Its floods have caused more deaths than any other natural disaster in history. In 1931, almost 4 million people died in a flood.

The name of a lake in Massachusetts has 45 letters. It was named Lake Chargogga-goggmanchauggagoggchaubunagungamaugg, which means "fishing place at the boundaries, neutral meeting grounds." The popular translation is: "You fish on your side, I fish on my side, nobody fishes in the middle."

Chapter 3

HEMISPHERE
North ↑
South ↓
East →
West ←

Land Sakes:
Fun Land and Nature Facts

If you were sailing in the Gulf of Guinea off the coast of Africa, you might enter four different hemispheres—north, south, east, and west—within 30 seconds.

At the Museo Inti-Nan in Ecuador, you can walk over the equator from one hemisphere into the other.

You weigh less on the equator than at other points on Earth.

In the United States, you can stand in one spot where four states intersect: Utah, Colorado, New Mexico, and Arizona.

The city of Panama on the Pacific side of the Panama Canal lies 25 miles (40 km) farther east than Colón, on the Atlantic side.

One point on Greenland is only 16 miles (26 km) from Canada.

Together, England, Scotland, and Ireland are smaller than the state of New Mexico in the United States.

Russia is the world's largest country. It is nearly double the size of China.

The world's tiniest country, Vatican City, is 0.2 square miles (0.52 sq km). It is located entirely within the city of Rome, Italy.

The world's southernmost trees grow on Tierra del Fuego, at the southernmost tip of South America. The world's northernmost trees are found on the Taymyr Peninsula in Siberia.

The largest living thing is General Sherman, a sequoia tree in Sequoia National Park, California. It is estimated to be between 3,000 and 4,000 years old. It stands 275 feet (84 m) tall. The trunk's circumference around the base is 83 feet 2 inches (25 m). This is roughly the same as 17 adults standing around it with arms outstretched, touching fingertips.

On the Isles of Scilly, only 28 miles (44.8 km) off the coast of England, palm trees, bananas, and other subtropical plants grow. None of these can grow in England.

Oak trees can withstand temperatures that are cold enough to kill banana and fig trees. But there is evidence that these three types of trees once grew side by side on the coast of North America.

The smallest trees in the world are the dwarf willows on Greenland's tundra. They are 2 inches (5 cm) high when full grown.

As the World Turns:
How Earth Has Changed

Many museums that feature the bones of animals have a resident colony of dermestid beetles. The beetles are used to clean carcasses completely, leaving only the clean skeletons. It takes the beetles about a week to polish off a large animal, and overnight for a small rodent or bat.

The earliest fossils are more than 3 billion years old.

There are about 900,000 species of insects in existence. Thousands of new ones are discovered each year.

At least 90 percent of all the species that have ever lived have become extinct.

All that remains of ancient monster sharks called megalodons are huge fossilized teeth. The shark was estimated to weigh 48 tons (43.2 metric tons), about the weight of seven large African elephants.

The Connecticut River Valley is home to one of the world's largest on-site displays of dinosaur tracks. Two thousand dinosaur footprints were found there.

In 1983, amateur fossil hunter Bill Walker found the claw of a dinosaur in Surrey, England. The claw was slightly smaller than the claw of a Tyrannosaurus Rex.

England's famous White Cliffs of Dover are made from the skeletons of microscopic sea animals piled one on top of another for billions of years.

The earliest ancestors of humans who walked upright and hunted for their food lived on Earth around 1.7 million years ago.

By 6000 B.C., the total human population on Earth was about 10 million. It is now 6.6 billion.

One of every five people on the planet Earth is Chinese. Every 24 hours there are about 22,000 to 27,000 more babies born in China, the most populous nation on Earth.

The world's most densely populated nation is Monaco. It is about the size of Central Park in New York City. It has a population of more than 32,000.

Greenland is 50 times larger than Denmark, which owns Greenland. However, Denmark has 97 times as many people.

The worst epidemic in the history of the human species was bubonic plague, also known as the "Black Death." In the 1300s, it killed one-third of the human population in Europe.

In the last 435 million years, there have been many huge catastrophes. These events have wiped out most of the life on Earth within a very short period of time. These periods are known as the "Great Dyings."

One catastrophe might have been one or more asteroids crashing into Earth. This caused a great cloud of debris that blocked the sunlight. Rocks at various sites around the world show an unusually high concentration of the element iridium, which is rare on Earth but abundant in asteroids.

Extreme changes in climate may have caused the extinction of the dinosaurs. A severe drop in temperature could have prevented eggs from being fertilized. This may have gone on long enough for the species to die out.

Come Rain or Shine:
Weather and Climate

Animals have been used to accurately predict the weather. Elks gather under sheltering trees two or three days before a blizzard. Fiddler crabs will burrow inland two days before a hurricane.

Weather is known to have an influence on human behavior. Sunshine results in increased activity on the New York Stock Exchange, while strong dry winds in Israel have a reputation for increasing human irritability.

Despite advanced technology, meteorologists can predict only one day's weather with reasonable accuracy.

We've learned about unusually cold European weather in the past through painters, not scientists. The paintings of Rembrandt van Rijn, Frans Hals, and Jan Vermeer (Dutch painters who lived in the 17th century) showed winter landscapes in which canals were frozen and snowdrifts rose to spectacular heights. Scientific evidence now proves what the painters showed us. There were severe winters for several years in that century.

Scientists are just as interested in "hindcasting" the weather as in forecasting it. This helps them learn about Earth's climate long ago.

The atmosphere is so sensitive to change that the climate can change drastically with even the slightest shift in the movement of continents or ocean currents.

Volcanoes can change our climate. For about two years following the 1991 eruption of Mount Pinatubo, average global temperatures decreased by approximately one degree.

Weather has played a major role in the development of civilizations. Whole groups of people, such as the Anasazi Indians of the American Southwest, died off or moved because of the lack of rain. Today, the Tuareg nomads, who live in the Sahara Desert and depend on their herds for milk, move around according to the pattern of rainfall.

In 1992, a lost 5,000-year-old empire was found along the Indus River in Pakistan. Today, it is known as the Mound of the Dead. It was probably abandoned because of floods.

When Egyptian soldiers saw rain for the first time, they thought it was a river falling from the sky.

The rainiest period anywhere on Earth was in Cherrapunji, India. In one year, from August 1860 to August 1861, there were 1,042 inches (2,647 cm) of rain.

In most parts of Chile, it rains almost every day. However, no rain has ever fallen in Calama, which is in the Desert of Atacama.

In Brussels, Belgium, it rains an average of 208 days a year.

A popular form of insurance in Europe is hailstone insurance. For generations, farmers have suffered extensive damage to property and crops from destructive hailstorms.

In 1888, a hailstorm in India killed about 250 people.

A single hailstone measured in the United States was 18.75 inches (47.6 cm) around. That's almost the same size as a soccer ball.

Chapter Five

In 1970, a hurricane off the coast of Bangladesh killed 300,000 people.

Cyclones rotate clockwise in the southern hemisphere and counterclockwise in the northern hemisphere.

Earth's air presses down on each of us with a force of 15 pounds (6.8 kg) per 1 square inch (6.5 sq. cm).

The energy in 10 minutes of one hurricane is equal to the power of all the nuclear weapons in the world.

During a tornado, the wind can move at 300 miles (480 km) per hour. Objects in its path can be totally destroyed, even exploding at the center. However, houses just to the side of its narrow path might be unharmed.

More tornadoes are reported in the United States than in any other country. About 800 to 1,200 occur every year.

Zimbabwe is one of the countries most often struck by lightning. In 1975, a single bolt of lightning killed 21 people who were taking shelter in a small hut.

Lightning is necessary for plant life. The intense heat of lightning forces nitrogen in the air to combine with oxygen, forming nitrogen oxides that are soluble in water and can fall to Earth as rain. Plants need nitrogen oxides to grow.

Here's a quick way to estimate how far away a storm is. Look for a flash of lightning and count the number of seconds before hearing the boom of thunder. Every five seconds equals 1 mile (1.6 km). So if you count 10 seconds, divide that by five and you will find the storm is 2 miles (3.2 km) away.

It never rains in Antarctica. All water comes down in the form of snow. Plant life on the continent is mostly mosses and lichens that cling to rocks.

Water, ice, and wind change the shape of the land like sculpting tools. A river can wear away a new course. Vast caves can be carved underground. Rock can be eroded and turned into sand. Mountains can be leveled. Hurricanes can wash tons of sand from beaches.

In one winter season from 1998 to 1999, 1,140 inches (2,896 cm) of snow fell at Mount Baker in Washington.

On February 18, 1979, snow fell on the Sahara Desert, in southern Algeria, for the first time in living memory. It lasted for half an hour and stopped traffic. It melted away within a few hours.

The Nile River flows through Africa, which is the world's warmest continent. The river froze over in the years 829 and 1010.

In a matter of two minutes, on the morning of January 22, 1943, the temperature in Spearfish, South Dakota, jumped from minus 4 F (minus 20 C) to 45 F (7.3 C).

The world's worst weather, a combination of wind, storms, cold, and ice, is believed to occur on top of New Hampshire's Mount Washington. It is at the meeting point of three storm tracks from the Arctic and the tropics. Wind has been recorded there at 231 miles (370 km) per hour. One hundred thirty-five people have died due to the extreme conditions.

The coldest temperature ever recorded on Earth was minus 129 F (minus 89 C). It was recorded on July 21, 1983, at 11,500 feet (3,508 m) above sea level at Russia's Vostok Station in Antarctica.

A warm summer's day at the South Pole may be minus 5 F (minus 20 C).

In wintertime, New York City can be colder than Iceland.

A manual issued to U.S. Navy personnel going to the Arctic or Antarctic reads: "Do not touch cold metal with moist, bare hands. If you should inadvertently stick a hand to cold metal, urinate on the metal to warm it and save some inches of skin."

The only state in the United States never to have recorded a temperature below 0 degrees Fahrenheit (minus 18 C) is Hawaii. The lowest temperature recorded there is 12 F (minus 11 C).

A person can freeze to death on the equator. However, you would have to be on top of Mount Kenya, which is 17,058 feet (5,203 m) high.

In Siberia, a person's breath freezes and crackles as it falls to the ground.

The northernmost city in the world is Hammerfest, Norway.

One of the northernmost points of land, Cape Morris Jesup on Greenland, is only 440 miles (704 km) from the North Pole.

Antarctica is the coldest place on Earth. It has an ice cap 3 miles (4.8 km) thick and temperatures recorded at more than minus 100 F (minus 73.9 C).

Up to 36 million years ago, Antarctica was a lot warmer. It was still joined to the southern tip of South America by a narrow strip of land. The small strip of land was enough to block the Antarctic current and send warmer water toward the South Pole.

After they died, earliest settlers in Greenland were buried deep in the soil. Later, people could be buried only near the surface because the ground was frozen. The cold has preserved the bodies to this day.

Until 1978, there was no native human population on Antarctica, and no child was ever born there. On January 7, 1978, a son was born to the wife of an Argentine army captain at the Argentine base in Antarctica.

When dinosaurs walked Earth, Greenland had a tropical climate. It was a warm place when Erik the Red and his Vikings discovered it and settled there 1,000 years ago. People raised cattle and sheep and grew grain. The weather began to change in 1200, making the land more inhospitable as time went by.

Glossary

ancestors—relatives who lived several generations ago

carcass—body of a dead animal

catastrophes—large disasters

civilization—a society that is highly developed

currents—parts of water that are moving along a path

cyclone—a storm with powerful winds

debris—litter

dikes—dams or high walls of earth built to hold back water from rivers, lakes, or seas

dune—a hill or ridge of sand piled up by the wind

equator—an imaginary line around the middle of Earth; it divides the northern and southern hemispheres

fossils—remains of plants or animals that lived long ago

glacier—a large sheet of slow-moving ice

gorge—a deep, narrow valley with steep, rocky walls

hemisphere—one half of Earth

hindcasting—looking at past weather to forecast the future

microscopic—so small that it can be seen only with a microscope

monsoon—a periodic wind in the Indian Ocean and southern Asia

plague—a serious disease that causes high rates of death

porous—full of holes

preserved—kept or saved from injury, loss, or ruin

salt deposit—an area of salt that is built up by a natural process

savanna—flat, grassy plain that has only a few trees

sea level—level of the surface of the sea used to measure heights and depths

submerged—beneath the water surface

topsoil—the layer of soil in which plants grow

updraft—an upward movement of air

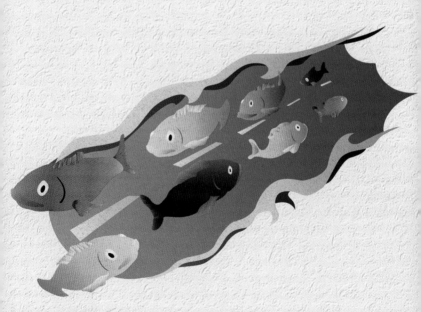

Index

To Learn More

More Books to Read

Berger, Melvin, and Gilda Berger. *Hurricanes Have Eyes but Can't See: and Other Amazing Facts About Wild Weather.* New York: Scholastic, 2003.

Fecher, Sarah, and Clare Oliver. *Freaky Facts About Natural Disasters.* Minnetonka, Minn.: Two-Can, 2006.

Seuling, Barbara. *Earth Is Like a Giant Magnet and Other Freaky Facts About Planets, Oceans, and Volcanoes.* Minneapolis: Picture Window Books, 2008.

On the Web

FactHound offers a safe, fun way to find Web sites related to topics in this book. All of the sites on FactHound have been researched by our staff.

1. Visit *www.facthound.com*
2. Type in this special code: 1404841172
3. Click on the FETCH IT button.

Your trusty FactHound will fetch the best sites for you!

Look for all of the books in the Freaky Facts series:

- Ancient Coins Were Shaped Like Hams and Other Freaky Facts About Coins, Bills, and Counterfeiting
- Cows Sweat Through Their Noses and Other Freaky Facts About Animal Habits, Characteristics, and Homes
- Earth Is Like a Giant Magnet and Other Freaky Facts About Planets, Oceans, and Volcanoes
- It Never Rains in Antarctica and Other Freaky Facts About Climate, Land, and Nature
- One President Was Born on Independence Day and Other Freaky Facts About the 26th through 43rd Presidents
- Some Porcupines Wrestle and Other Freaky Facts About Animal Antics and Families
- There Are Millions of Millionaires and Other Freaky Facts About Earning, Saving, and Spending
- Three Presidents Died on the Fourth of July and Other Freaky Facts About the First 25 Presidents
- You Blink Twelve Times a Minute and Other Freaky Facts About the Human Body
- Your Skin Weighs More Than Your Brain and Other Freaky Facts About Your Skin, Skeleton, and Other Body Parts